KINGDOM BUSINESS: LICENSED TO LEAD

Journey Journal

KEVIN SUBER

Copyright © 2019 Kevin Suber
All rights reserved.

ISBN 13: 9781698184548

"The pessimist complains about the wind. The optimist expects it to change. The leader adjusts the sails."

—**John Maxwell**

I know what I'm doing. I have it all planned out—plans to take care of you, not abandon you, plans to give you the future you hope for.

Jeremiah 19:11
The Message (MSG).

KINGDOM BUILDING

1) Which definition of Kingdom is closest to how you define Kingdom? Why?

2) How do you define Kingdom?

3) If you had your choice of any Kingdom (Monarchial, Sports Dynasty, Business, Country, Heaven, etc.) that ever existed or will exist—which would you choose and why?

4) Are you MAD? What made you MAD? What do you need to be ready to make a difference (MAD)?

5) Are you intimidated by or afraid of building your Kingdom?

6) Do you believe you can build your Kingdom? How satisfied will you be by building your Kingdom?

7) If you had unlimited resources, what Kingdom would you build?

8) What resources do you need to build your Kingdom?

Notes

Notes

Notes

GIFTS AND TALENTS

1) What task or activity is effortless for you?

2) Do people seek your help with a specific task or activity?

3) Have you ever been called gifted or talented? What gift or talent do people point to?

4) What do you believe your gift(s) is/are?

5) If you have more than one gift—which is your favorite and why?

6) What is/are your talent(s)?

7) Do your gifts and/or talents make you overwhelmed or afraid?

8) What is stopping you from utilizing your gifts and talents?

Notes

Notes

Notes

YOUR *WHY*

1) Have you ever woken up in the morning but did not feeling like getting out of bed?

2) How do you/did you overcome that feeling?

3) What is your *Why*? Who makes you want to be better? What cause is so massive or dire or it breaks your heart . . . makes you cry because it MUST change?

4) What is a cause that you would give up anything for? Why?

5) Who would you do anything for? Why?

6) Does the thought of not having success make you anxious or does it help you to focus?

Notes

Notes

Notes

VISION

1) What are you grateful for?

2) Do you have a hard time seeing good things in your life? Is it hard to find things to be grateful for?

3) Are there people in your life who discount the good in your life? Are there people in your life who distract you from your gratefulness? Are there people in your life who hinders you from achieving greatness?

4) What are you passionate about? What excites you?

5) What task/deed/project do you think about often? What is your most frequent thought?

6) Do you feel like you're running out of time?

7) If your gifts and talents were perfected what would you do?

8) If you had no financial concerns - what would you be doing right now?

9) Do you feel at peace, in general?

10) What does your perfect future look like?

Notes

Notes

Notes

EXECUTION

1) Do you fear that you will not be able to execute your vision? Why?

2) Have you ever had a vision and tried to execute it? Did you succeed, delay, or stop?

3) What have you learned from previous failed attempts to executing your vision (or past projects)? List them.

4) Who, in your life, inspires and supports your vision?

5) Who in your life speaks negatively about your vision?

6) Summarize the four steps of execution.

7) What is the most challenging part(s) of execution for you?

8) Who or what can help you overcome this challenge?

9) What is preventing you from the execution of your project or vision?

10) Are you ready to execute your vision?

11) Do you believe you can execute your vision?

Notes

Notes

Notes

LEADERSHIP

1) Are you a leader? Why or why not?

2) Whom do you consider to be a great leader?

3) What characteristics do you believe a good leader should possess?

4) If you could spend an afternoon with anyone, from past or present, who would you spend it with in order to be a better leader? Why?

5) Do you consider yourself an expert in any area?

6) How much time do you spend on self-improvement?

7) What do you wish you could spend more time doing?

8) Who do you spend the most time with? Which leaders in your life do you spend time with?

9) What do you do when you're running out of time?

10) Do you have a mentor or a mentee? Both?

11) Name a challenge from your past that prevented you from starting a project or from growing.

Notes

Notes

Notes

ALL TOGETHER NOW—MY VIEW ON LEADERSHIP BY J. TODD HARRIS

I've worked most of my life in creative endeavors—primarily theatre and film as a producer. So much of my experience has either been with creative leaders, such as directors, or business leaders, including investors and other producers.

I realized in high school and college that if I wanted certain things to happen, I probably had to instigate them and if I wanted them to happen at their best level, I had to follow through, often including undertaking tasks that others weren't interested in (e.g. raising money). During high school, I started a school newspaper because there wasn't one and I liked having a platform for self-expression. In college, when I wanted to be in a certain musical, I realized I had to make it happen. Then to make sure it worked, I had to maintain my focus on executing it. So, I wasn't in it, but I took great joy from making it happen and entertaining a theatre crowd bursting at the seams. It was an experience and I loved "creating" it. It became my drug of choice. It was in those early days that I realized that producing meant starting with nothing and then—hopefully—ending up with a theatre full of cheering people. It was satisfying. And I've never looked back; only sought new and interesting ways to achieve that same feeling. I believe being happy—making a product you like—makes you a better leader, or at least makes it easier for you to be a better leader.

Leaders I respect, have a vision, are able to share that vision, inspire others to support it, and instill a conviction in those participating that the enterprise has value and their participation has merit. And, then, finally, once the goal has been realized, celebrate the achievement in a shared manner. In my experience, while it's important to feel good about ourselves—most of us have healthy egos—what really matters is the accomplishment. And if it takes sharing the glory or even directing the glory to others, what matters is the end result. Because isn't that what we sought to begin with? It's like a team sport—the whole team can celebrate and the coach has the satisfaction of knowing he orchestrated it.

I have a quip about producing; I've probably delivered 500 times. I love producing because you don't need to have any discernible skills. You get to work with all these people with specific talents that you don't have and then you get to take credit for it. Of course, that's a gross simplification, but there is more than a grain of truth in it. I'm not a writer, director, designer, editor, cinematographer—yet I'm a "filmmaker." Of course, I greatly value what these artists contribute to the creative process because without them, we'd have no creative achievement to celebrate.

My "art" turns out to be bringing people together and getting them to work in harmony. Hopefully.

At this point, I've produced over 45 movies and dozens of stage productions. My job has always been to give the process credibility, create an environment in which art will hopefully flourish, to make sure that art reaches as much audience as possible and to try to make a return for risk capital. Ideally, producers have very symbiotic relationships with artists. And I believe that same relationship applies to leadership, in general. Everyone has to benefit. Strong leaders facilitate an environment in which people feel valued and get to share the overall accomplishment. And good leaders are strategic, reliable, and relentless.

J. Todd Harris
Producer/Filmmaker

EMBRACING LEADERSHIP BY DR. VIKKI JOHNSON

The moment I recognized and embraced myself as a leader was during my childhood. At the age of ten, I started my first girls' club. Our name was the "Clover Zodiacs". The membership consisted of family members, school friends, and neighborhood buddies. We wrote a theme song, went on weekend excursions, and did community service— what is most beautiful is that we are still friends more than forty years later.

    I recognized very early my gift to influence people, create powerful relationships, and edify others to become their best. This knack for leadership was nurtured through sports. In middle and high school as well as college, I was the captain of the volleyball and basketball teams. I was a "student leader" who loved teamwork to make dreams work. The confidence I gained from my coaches and advisors and parents entrusting me with such responsibility only served to fortify and reinforce that I was indeed a leader.

    As an adult, my leadership capacity has continued to grow. I now lead a community of other women leaders who look to me for guidance as they lead others. It is an awesome privilege from God, to be able to serve the emerging leaders, cultivate their potential, and affirm what they already know. Great leaders are phenomenal followers, lifetime students, teachable, humble, and perpetually grateful.

Dr. Vikki Johnson
Creator, Soul Wealth
www.vikkijohnson.com

THE IMPORTANCE OF LEADERSHIP
BY DAN OH

There are so many tentacles to the concept of leadership, but with a decade of leadership experience, whether on the job, in the church, or with my own family, I have arrived at a few notions that I think sum up what makes an amazing leader.

The Best Leader Is a Servant Leader. True leadership is a principle that starts and ends with the heart. Influencing people to be their best selves and constantly challenging them to persevere through tough circumstances takes a pure and genuine heart.

We are taught to excel above people, push past people, and cut each other down if it means we will get ahead. But we will never reach new heights if we keep chopping down the proverbial tree. We must serve and lift others up and have faith that these same individuals reciprocate from the heart . . . not just to those who serve them, but to others. That is how change reverberates—with selflessness, the spirit to live for others, and the clear understanding that joy comes from seeing others do well. This not only breeds great energy, but it also unites people under the established goal, giving them the willingness to suffer together in order to succeed.

In the immortal words of Chris McCandless, "Happiness is real when shared." Sharing manifests through service.

How Do You Not Lose the Forest for the Tress? With Trust. The path to leadership begins with understanding how the designated work is done and what it takes to accomplish the task(s) at hand.

Leadership, in its essence, is about trust. Trust that the values, skills, and knowledge you've bestowed on those who work with you and for you will be set into motion. Trust that those same individuals will want to do their very, very best for you because you've inspired them with something more than raises, promotions, and short-lived incentives. Trust that holding a group together takes a higher power and that if it's a righteous endeavor, that power is accounted for.

Work from the heart, and you will always have the capacity to see the bigger picture, you will gain wisdom to shape your vision, and you will develop the flexibility to adjust accordingly. Trees are beautiful, but a panoramic view of the forest is breathtaking.

Be Transformational, Not Transactional. The ones who can help carry out your vision are getting younger by the day. The reality—the most influential sector of our workforce is our Millennials, and soon, our Generation Z community. This is a demographic that has amassed such a breadth of knowledge about their own places in society, the ins and outs of their career path, and more tools than ever to make their dreams come true.

How do we harness the verve, passion, and savviness of this generation? We provide them opportunities to transform themselves. It goes beyond salary, career path creation, or benefits packages. They must understand that in exchange for their time, skills, and professionalism, they will be given chances to create effective and lasting change . . . in the least, they will have a better shot at achieving their personal goals through you. Compensation packages will not satisfy. To effectively lead these young people, they need to understand that they will be able to maximize their youth and become more well-rounded individuals under your tutelage and guidance.

There's no way around it—being a leader means either transforming those who follow you or die trying. This new and dynamic workforce will give you results beyond what you could ever expect.

Dan Oh
Marketing Director
International Youth Fellowship, USA

OVERCOMING CHALLENGES

1) Have you ever experienced death or any other crisis (Health Challenges, Divorce, Bankruptcy, Floods, etc.) in your life?

2) Name an incident or a challenge from your past that paralyzed you.

3) Did this challenge make you feel like tomorrow would not arrive?

4) What happened? Have you assessed what actually happened during this incident?

5) How did you "pivot" from what happened?

6) What did you learn from this (these) crisis(es)? Name three or more things that you learned.

7) What will you do when you face your next challenge?

Notes

Notes

Notes

LEGACY

1) If your legacy was your leadership are you satisfied to leave that example for generations to come?

2) What would you add, subtract, or change to make your leadership an acceptable legacy?

3) Do you feel like you're running out of time to leave your legacy?

4) What do you want to leave behind for the benefit of others?

5) Which of your gifts and talents will be needed to establish your legacy?

6) Who has different gifts and talents that are different from yours that can help you accomplish this? Who can help in your mission? How will you put your efforts to leave a lasting impact?

7) Who will benefit from this legacy that you leave?

8) History has its eyes on you. Does that change your perspective on the legacy that you will leave?

Notes

Notes

Notes

Made in the USA
Monee, IL
01 February 2023